Thinker Doodles
Half 'n Half Animals A1

Think, Draw & Color

SERIES TITLES
Beginning Clues & Choose
Clues & Choose A1
Half 'n Half Animals A1
Half 'n Half Animals B1

Created By
Elaine Heller

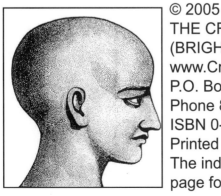

© 2005
THE CRITICAL THINKING CO.
(BRIGHT MINDS™)
www.CriticalThinking.com
P.O. Box 1610 • Seaside • CA 93955
Phone 800-458-4849 • Fax 831-393-3277
ISBN 0-89455-867-6
Printed in the United States of America

Skills Developed in This Book

Critical Thinking (Analysis, Synthesis)

Observation

Hand-eye Coordination

Spatial Awareness

Fine Motor Development

Directionality

Symmetry

Vocabulary

TEACHING SUGGESTIONS: Each activity in this book asks children to identify and draw information missing in a simple line drawing of an animal. Children are then asked to color the completed picture using their creative imagination, not just the expected colors.

Teachers and parents are encouraged to extend the activity by involving children in discussions about each animal: facts, sounds, colors.

Level A Book 1 is composed of four uniquely different sections. The first section requires children to draw the missing parts in animal faces only. Section II introduces the concept of symmetry in "Half 'N Half" drawings. This section will help develop skills needed to complete the more challenging activities in sections III and IV.

Dedication

This book is dedicated to my two grandsons, Ryan and Bradley Heller, who love to go to the zoo and see all the different kinds of animals. They, along with a neighbor's children, Erin, Audrey, and Ian, share my love of animals and have provided creative ideas of many of my drawings.

Thanks to all the children who have tried my animal drawings, from my former art students at Brookline Elementary, Houston Independent School District to many others I have had contact with and who have inspired me. The genuine enthusiasm of all these children and students has inspired me to continue to create these drawings for more children to experience.

From my first book, Half 'n Half Design and Color, to this latest endeavor using the same concept with animals, it has been a worthwhile and satisfying endeavor.

Elaine Heller

Table of Contents

MOUSE

I like to eat cheese!

Draw the missing parts of the picture, then color the picture. Can you add something else to the picture?

PART II

ANIMAL FACES

Children are now able to draw more of the animal's face. Parts are still missing, but dots now replace one side of the face—either the left or the right. The dots act as clues in drawing. Helping the child observe the symmetry in the given half of the drawing will act as a valuable tool in developing skills used in spatial awareness.

The "S" on the drawing stands for START and indicates the starting point to complete the drawing. LEFT and RIGHT appear at the top but disappear after the CHIMPANZEE. Simple facts about the animals continue through this segment.

PENGUIN

LEFT   RIGHT

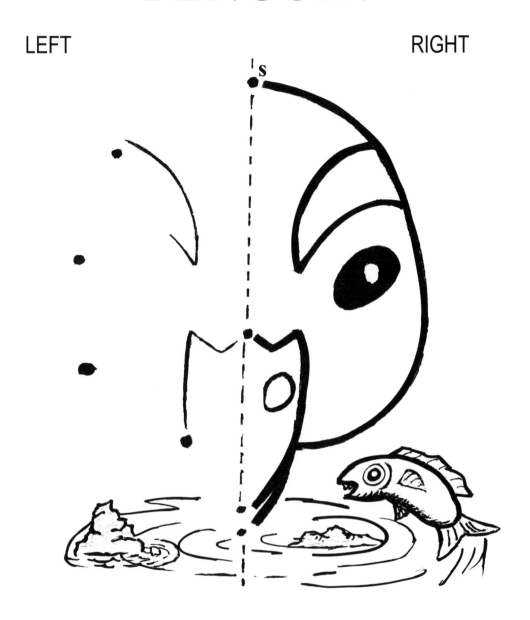

I live at the North Pole
where it is icy and cold.

Draw the missing parts of the picture, then color the
picture. Can you add something else to the picture?

LIONESS

LEFT   RIGHT

My home is in Africa where I am
a very good hunter.

Draw the missing parts of the picture, then color the
picture. Can you add something else to the picture?

FROG

LEFT   RIGHT

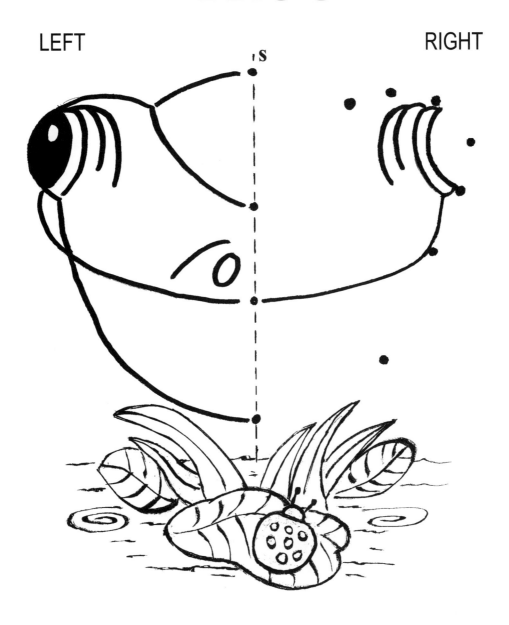

I am a very good jumper.

Draw the missing parts of the picture, then color the picture. Can you add something else to the picture?

HIPPOPOTAMUS

LEFT   RIGHT

You can find me peeking up out of the
water in rivers or lakes.

Draw the missing parts of the picture, then color the
picture. Can you add something else to the picture?

CHIMPANZEE

LEFT   RIGHT

I live in the jungle and love to
swing in the trees.

Draw the missing parts of the picture, then color the
picture. Can you add something else to the picture?

CROCODILE

I am a reptile with sharp teeth.
I live by lakes and rivers.

Draw the missing parts of the picture, then color the
picture. Can you add something else to the picture?

RABBIT

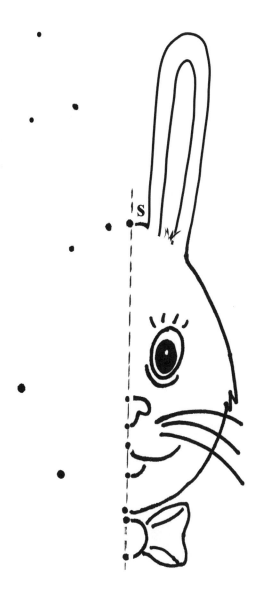

Hopping is what I do. What food do
you think I like best?

Draw the missing parts of the picture, then color the
picture. Can you add something else to the picture?

OWL

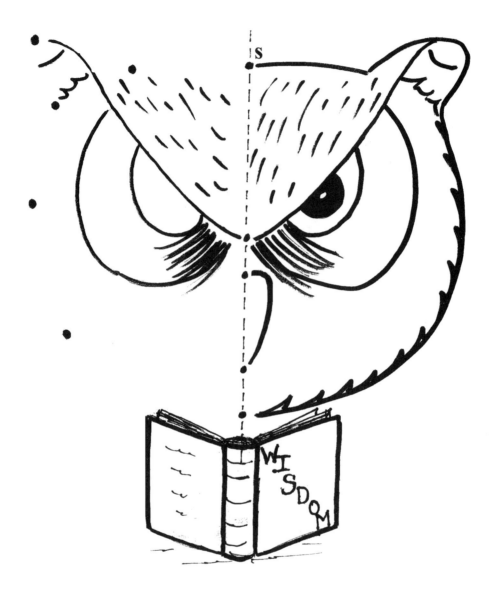

I am known as a wise owl.

Draw the missing parts of the picture, then color the picture. Can you add something else to the picture?

LION

I am king of the jungle.

Draw the missing parts of the picture,
then color the picture.
Can you draw my mane like this?
Can you add something else to the
picture?

BILLY GOAT

I am a male goat and will grow horns.
I like to eat grass and clover.

Draw the missing parts of the picture, then color the picture. Can you add something else to the picture?

PART III

FRONT VIEW OF BODY

A new element is added in this section. Children are introduced to the partial or full body of the animal facing forward and will apply the same concept as in PART II; dots act as clues in completing the missing half. More spatial judgment is needed to complete this section. Drawings have LEFT and RIGHT at the top of the page.

COCKER SPANIEL PUPPY

LEFT   RIGHT

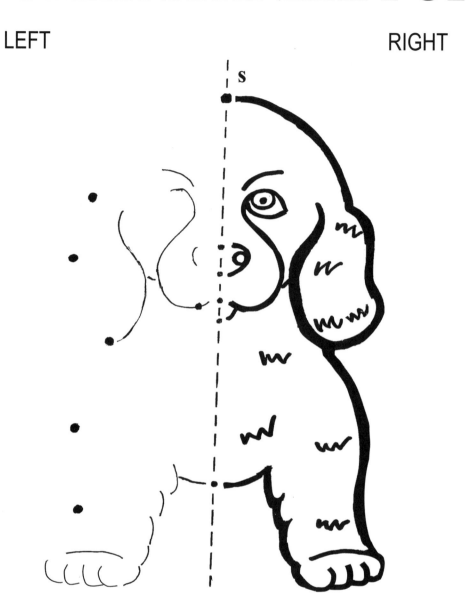

Chewing on your shoe makes me happy!

Draw the missing parts of the picture,
then color the picture.
Can you make my fur like this?
Can you add something else to the
picture?

ELEPHANT

LEFT   RIGHT

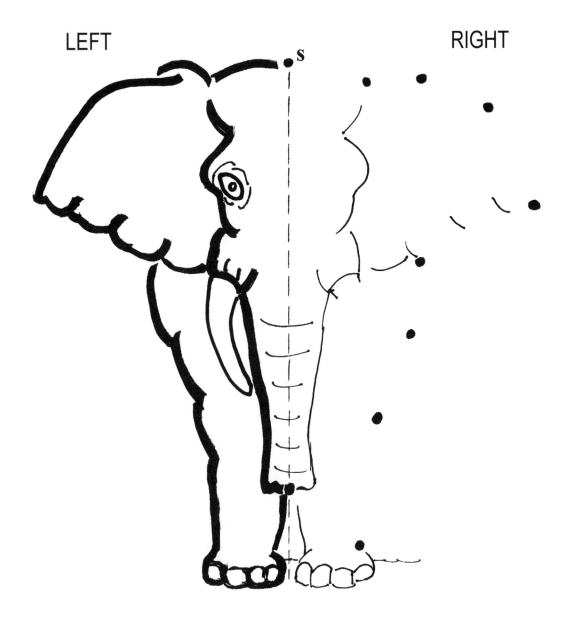

I am very big and strong. My
long trunk helps me eat, drink,
and breathe.

Draw the missing parts of the picture, then color the
picture. Can you add something else to the picture?

PENGUIN

LEFT   RIGHT

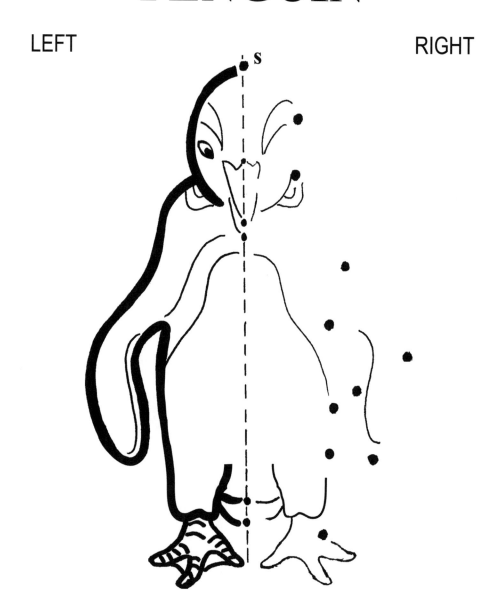

You'll find me in the icy cold of the
Antarctic. I eat lots of fish.

Draw the missing parts of the picture, then color the
picture. Can you add something else to the picture?

SHAGGY DOG

LEFT   RIGHT

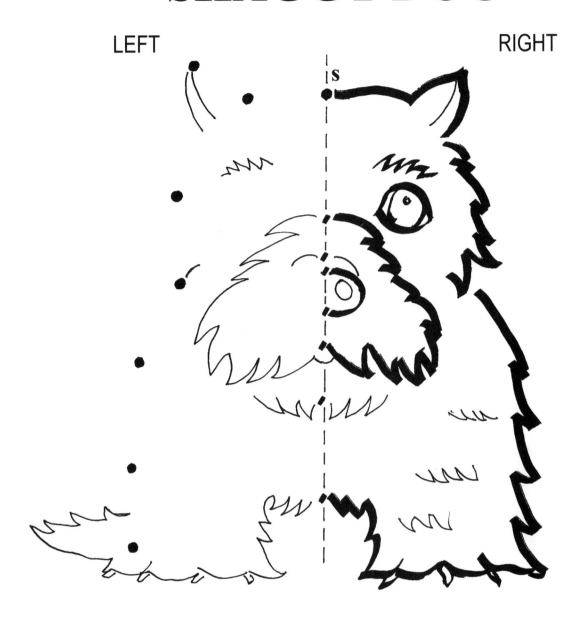

My fur is very thick and shaggy.

Draw the missing parts of the
picture, then color the picture.
Can you make this line?
Can you add something else
to the picture?

SHEEP

LEFT   RIGHT

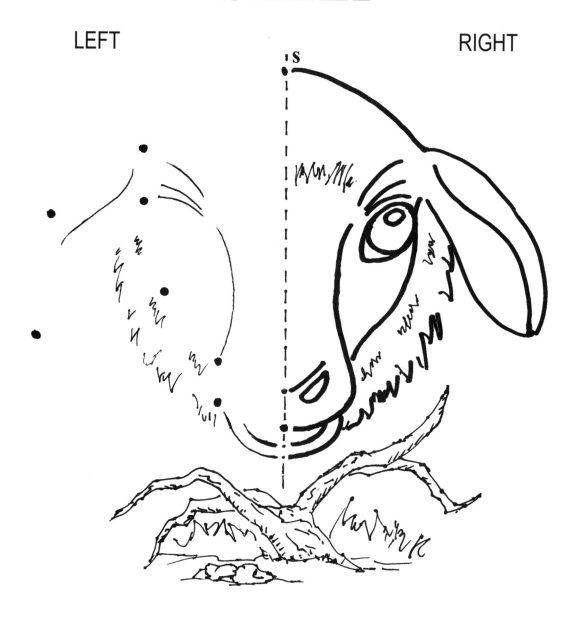

I live on a grassy field. My soft wool
is used to make yarn for clothing.

Draw the missing parts of the picture, then color the
picture. Can you add something else to the picture?

PART IV

FRONT VIEW OF BODY

This section goes one step further and includes questions that suggest additional background drawing for each animal. Teachers and parents are encouraged to give little, if any, direction to the student. This is a great opportunity to let the child explore "outside the box" thinking!

HORSE

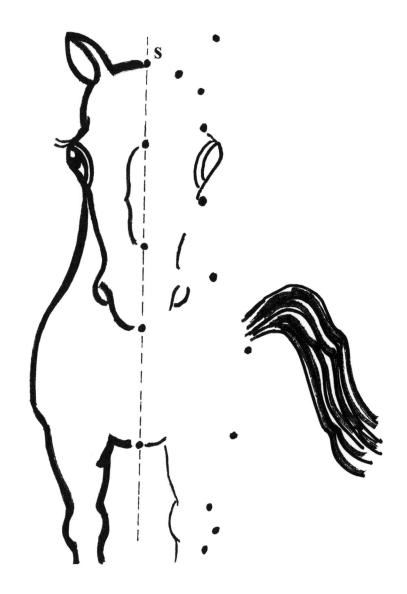

I live on a farm and like to eat
grass and hay.

Draw the missing parts of the picture, then color the
picture. Can you add something else to the picture?

BEAR CUB

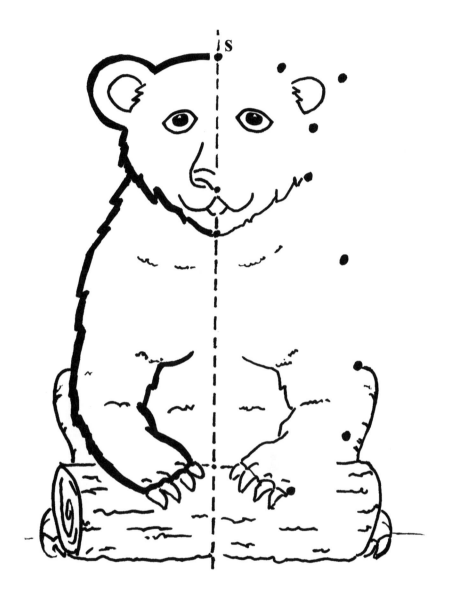

I will get very big when I grow up.

Draw the missing parts of the picture, then color the picture. Can you draw a tree for me to climb? Can you add something else to the picture?

KOALA

I am a marsupial and live in trees all my life.

Draw the missing parts of the picture, then color the picture. Can you draw what you think my home looks like? Can you add something else to the picture?

FROG

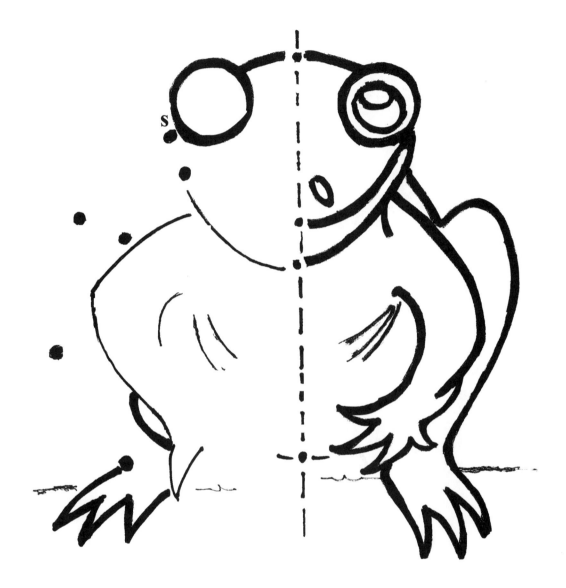

I am an amphibian. I am born
in water but later live on land.

Draw the missing parts of the picture, then color the
picture. Can you draw some tall grass and flowers
next to me? Can you add something else to the
picture?

DAIRY COW

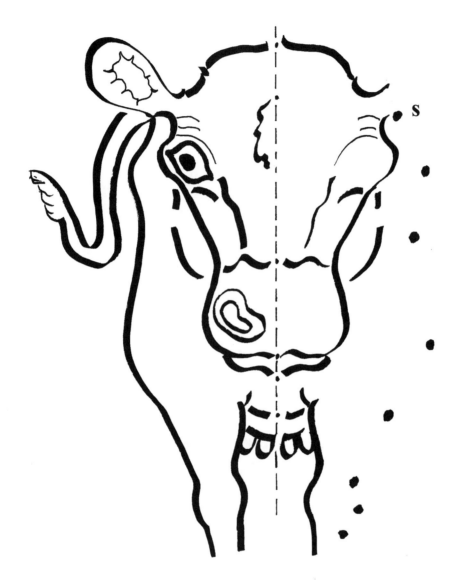

The milk for your cereal comes
from me.

Draw the missing parts of the picture, then color the picture. Can you draw my right side and my other ear, eye,
and nostril? Can you add something else to the picture?

RHINOCEROS

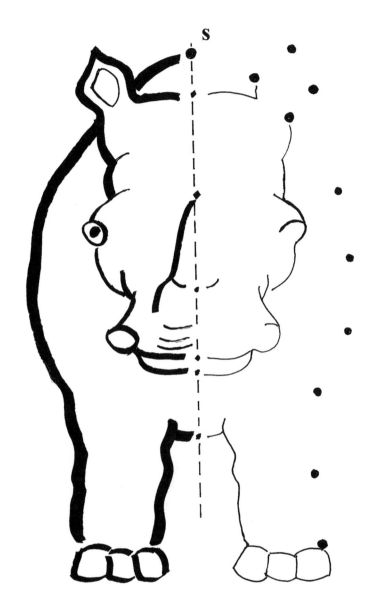

I have a sharp horn in the middle of my face.

Draw the missing parts of the picture, then color the picture. Can you draw a horn for me? Can you add something else to the picture?

SEAL CUB

I live in Alaska and have a smooth and
shiny skin. I like to float on ice.

Draw the missing parts of the picture, then color the
picture. Can you draw some mountains in back?
Can you add something else to the picture?

CHICK

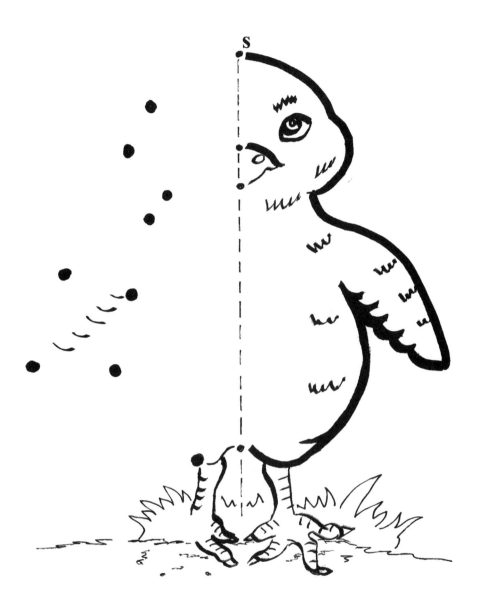

My feathers are very soft and yellow. I
hatch from an egg.

Draw the missing parts of the picture, then color the
picture. Can you draw some kernels of corn for my
dinner? Can you add something else to the picture?

HIPPOPOTAMUS

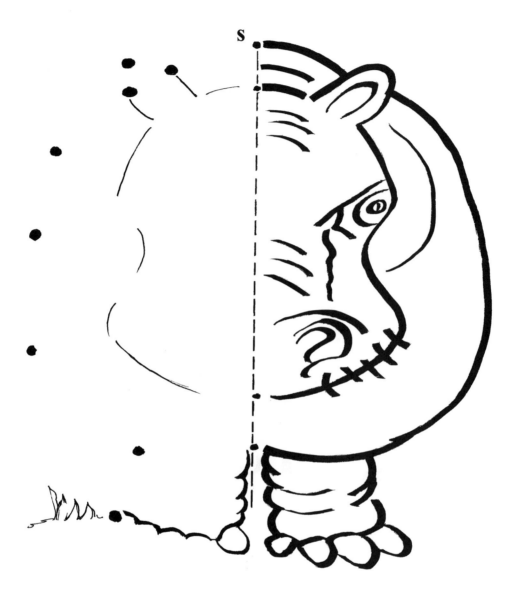

I am a big round shape.

Draw the missing parts of the picture, then color the picture. Can you add something else to the picture?

CAT

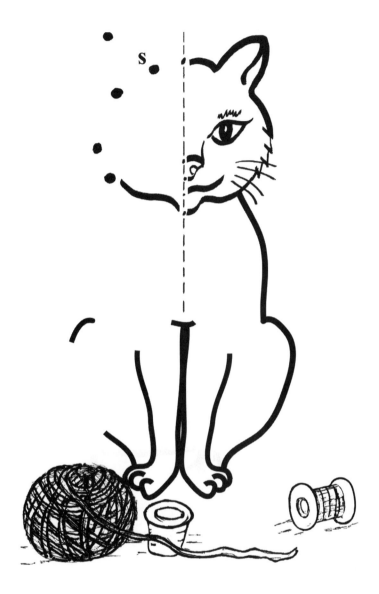

I like to play with all kinds of things, including mice!

Draw the missing parts of the picture, then color the picture. Can you draw my tail? Can you add something else to the picture?

REINDEER

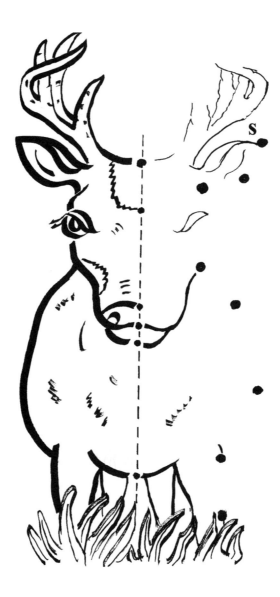

I help pull Santa's sled.

Draw the missing parts of the picture, then color the picture. Can you draw the missing parts of my antlers? Can you add something else to the picture?

TURTLE

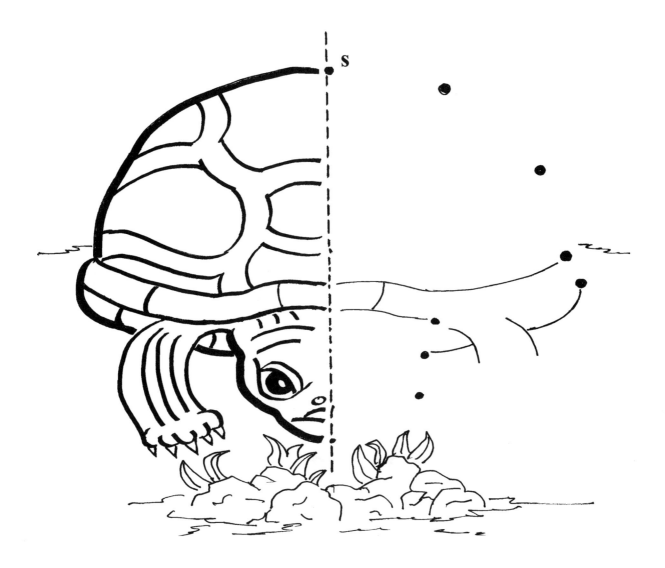

I am a reptile and my children hatch
from small eggs.

Draw the missing parts of the picture, then color the
picture. Can you draw little turtles around me? Can
you add something else to the picture?

ZEBRA

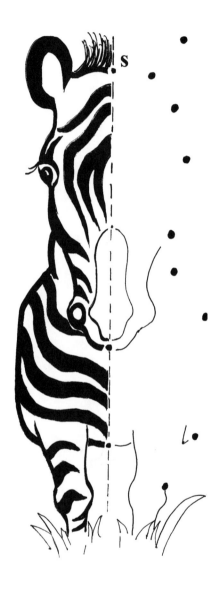

I live in Africa. My stripes make a
beautiful pattern.

Draw the missing parts of the picture, then color the
picture. Can you draw trees to give me shade? Can
you add something else to the picture?

LEOPARD

I live in the jungle, and my spots help me hide
in trees and bushes.

Draw the missing parts of the picture, then color the
picture. Can you draw more spots on me? Can you
add something else to the picture?

GIRAFFE

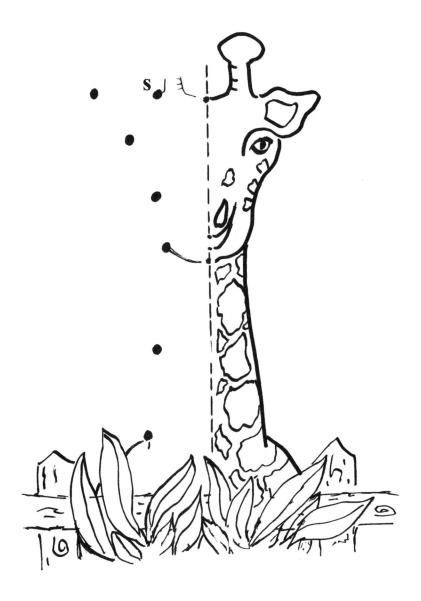

I am very tall, with the longest
neck of all the animals.

Draw the missing parts of the picture, then color the
picture. Can you draw a tall tree with some tender
leaves for me? Can you add something else to the
picture?